T0204993

Who Was
Thomas
Jefferson?

Who Was Thomas Jefferson?

by Dennis Brindell Fradin

illustrated by John O'Brien

Penguin Workshop

For Tess—JO'B

PENGUIN WORKSHOP
An Imprint of Penguin Random House LLC, New York

Text copyright © 2003 by Dennis Brindell Fradin.
Illustrations copyright © 2003 by John O'Brien. Cover illustration copyright © 2003 by Penguin Random House LLC. All rights reserved.
Published by Penguin Workshop, an imprint of Penguin Random House LLC, New York.
PENGUIN and PENGUIN WORKSHOP are trademarks of Penguin Books Ltd.
WHO HQ & Design is a registered trademark of Penguin Random House LLC.
Printed in the USA.

Visit us online at www.penguinrandomhouse.com.

Library of Congress Control Number: 2003005232

ISBN 9780448431451   45 44 43 42 41

Contents

Who Was
Thomas Jefferson?

Thomas Jefferson is pictured on U.S. nickels. He is also portrayed on the giant Mount Rushmore sculpture in South Dakota. The Jefferson Memorial is a popular landmark in Washington, D.C. Jefferson City, Missouri, and Mount Jefferson in Oregon are among the many places named for him.

JEFFERSON MEMORIAL

Why is Thomas Jefferson honored in all these ways?

He wrote the Declaration of Independence. This paper announced the birth of the United States in 1776. Its stirring words, such as "all men are created equal," have inspired people for almost 250 years.

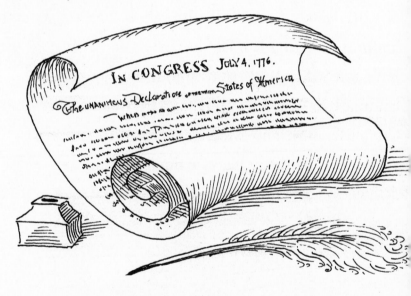

Jefferson was a giant in many fields. A great statesman, he was our third President. A gifted architect, he designed Virginia's statehouse and the

University of Virginia campus. People called him "Mr. Mammoth" because he collected prehistoric bones. His book collection became the core of the Library of Congress.

Despite his many public triumphs, Jefferson's private life was often sad. His wife, Martha, died at the age of only thirty-three. Only two of Thomas and Martha's six children lived to adulthood. Jefferson also felt guilty that he didn't live by his own words. The man who wrote, "all men are created equal," also enslaved hundreds of people, and believed that black people were inferior to white people. And toward the end of his life, the former President landed deeply in debt.

This is the true story of a man with many sides: Thomas Jefferson.

Chapter 1
Tall Tom

Thomas Jefferson was born in 1743 on his family's plantation, Shadwell, in central Virginia. Virginia was one of thirteen colonies belonging to Great Britain. By the calendar used then, his birth date was April 2. By today's calendar his birth date was April 13.

Tom came third in a family of ten children. Two of the children didn't survive infancy. So Tom grew up with two older sisters, four younger sisters, and a younger brother. The babies of the family, Anna and Randolph, were twins.

Little is known about Tom's mother, Jane Randolph Jefferson. Far more is known about his father. Peter Jefferson was a prosperous farmer who owned dozens of slaves. He was also a

THE THIRTEEN COLONIES

SHADWELL

surveyor, a person who measures land boundaries. In addition, he served in Virginia's legislature. Young Tom thought his father was the smartest

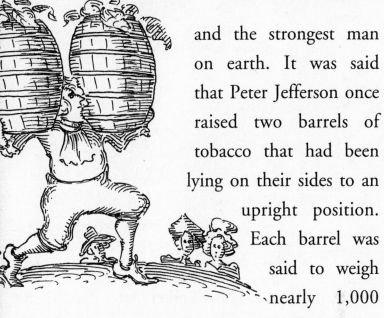

and the strongest man on earth. It was said that Peter Jefferson once raised two barrels of tobacco that had been lying on their sides to an upright position. Each barrel was said to weigh nearly 1,000 pounds. He also loved books and read Shakespeare and other authors in his spare time.

Tom had cousins named Randolph, who lived in eastern Virginia. Mr. and Mrs. Randolph died

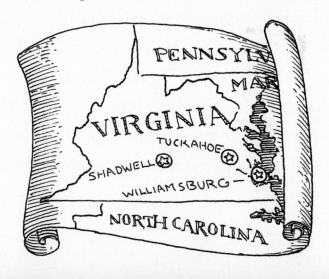

within a few years of each other. After that, Tom's parents helped raise the three Randolph children. Tom's first memory was of moving to his cousins' home, about fifty miles away, when he was two. For much of his childhood, Tom went back and forth between the two places. Sometimes he was home at Shadwell. Other times he and his family were at Tuckahoe, the Randolph estate.

In a way, Tom had the best of two worlds. At Shadwell, which stood at the edge of the wilderness, his father taught him to ride, swim, fish, and

hunt. In eastern Virginia, Tom went to dances and learned to dress and behave like an English gentleman. But he apparently didn't get along with his Randolph cousins. The boy cousin, also named Tom, was two years older and seems to have bullied him.

When Tom Jefferson was nine, someone else took charge of his cousins. Most of the Jefferson family returned to Shadwell. But to his disappointment,

when his family went home in 1752, Tom was sent to study with Reverend William Douglas, near Tuckahoe.

Reverend Douglas taught Tom Latin, Greek, and French. Tom studied and lived with Reverend Douglas for five years. The only time he returned to Shadwell was for vacations. Although his schoolwork often bored him, Tom liked to read on his own. He became so wrapped up in books that he sometimes read for fifteen hours straight.

Young Tom also loved music. He practiced his violin three hours a day.

By age thirteen, Tom was a tall, thin, redheaded boy with freckles. He was well on his way to his full height of six feet two inches. In an age when the average man stood five feet six inches tall, Tom was almost a giant. His nickname was "Tall Tom."

Tom was home for the summer of 1757 when his father became ill. Peter Jefferson

died that August. Fourteen-year-old Tom was crushed to lose his father and hero. As the oldest son, Tom inherited much of his father's estate, including about 2,500 acres of land and about thirty slaves. But he wasn't to receive the bulk of his inheritance until he turned twenty-one.

Peter Jefferson had wanted Tom to go to college. To prepare for it, Tom lived and studied with another minister for two more years. He didn't much like this teacher, either. But at least he was now close enough to Shadwell to spend weekends at home. By 1760, "Tall Tom" was sixteen years old and eager to begin college.

Chapter 2
Tall Tom in Love

Tom moved to Williamsburg in the spring of 1760. This city near the coast was Virginia's capital and home to the College of William and Mary. Tom loved college from the start. He was hungry for knowledge and enjoyed studying late into the night.

One professor, William Small, befriended him. In turn, Dr. Small introduced him to his friends George Wythe and Francis Fauquier. Wythe was a noted lawyer. Fauquier was the colonial governor of Virginia for Great Britain.

COLLEGE OF WILLIAM AND MARY

Fauquier often invited Small, Wythe, and Jefferson to dine at the Governor's Palace. Sometimes the red haired college student played his violin at concerts hosted by the governor.

Tom graduated in 1762 after just two years. Now he had to think about a career. Law appealed to him. In those days, young men (there were no women lawyers yet) studied with established attorneys. After a while, the young men took a law test. Those who passed, became lawyers.

Tom began studying under George Wythe. He couldn't have had a better teacher. In colonial days, lawyers generally had poor reputations. A few colonies even had laws preventing lawyers from entering their borders! Wythe, however, was famous for his honesty. If he thought a person was in the wrong or lying, he wouldn't take the case.

Wythe did not go easy on Tom, even though they were friends. Tom studied with George Wythe for five years. In comparison, Tom's friend Patrick Henry studied for just several months before becoming a lawyer. Even today, law schools generally require just three years of study. One reason for Tom's lengthy preparation was that Wythe was a treasury of legal knowledge. Another was that Tom liked his law teacher. He called Wythe, who was seventeen years older than himself, "my second father."

In 1767, Jefferson was admitted to the bar. He began to practice law near Shadwell as well as in the capital city of Williamsburg. George Wythe had taught Tom well. His first year, the twenty-four-year-old attorney handled sixty-seven cases. This grew to 115 cases his second year, and about 200 his third year. Tom's problem was that he didn't press his clients to pay him. In his first six years as an attorney, Tom collected only a third of his fees!

Tom also became interested in politics. In 1769 he ran for and won a seat in the House of Burgesses. This was Virginia's legislature. It was America's oldest lawmaking body made up of elected representatives. Jefferson served in the House of Burgesses until the American Revolution ended colonial government.

HOUSE OF BURGESSES

THE VIRGINIA HOUSE OF BURGESSES MET TO DECIDE LOCAL LAWS. ITS HISTORIC FIRST MEETING TOOK PLACE AT JAMESTOWN IN 1619.

THE HOUSE OF BURGESSES PLAYED A KEY ROLE IN THE AMERICAN REVOLUTION. IN THE 1760S AND 1770S, ITS MEMBERS BEGAN TO CHALLENGE DECISIONS MADE BY THE ROYAL GOVERNOR OF VIRGINIA. THE BURGESSES, AS THEY WERE CALLED, HELPED SPUR A UNIFIED FIGHT FOR FREEDOM THROUGHOUT THE THIRTEEN COLONIES.

Law and politics weren't the only things on his mind. His family's home, Shadwell, burned down in 1770. Jefferson was in Charlottesville, Virginia, when a slave brought the news. After learning that his relatives were safe, Jefferson asked if all the property was lost.

"Not all," the slave answered. "We saved your fiddle."

The year of the fire, Jefferson began building a new home that he had designed. Using slave labor, the thirty-five-room mansion was built on a hilltop four miles from Shadwell and also near the town of Charlottesville. He called his new estate Monticello. The name means *little mountain* in Italian.

Young ladies were also in his thoughts. At nineteen, he had fallen in love with sixteen-year-old Rebecca Burwell. Tom carried a silhouette of Rebecca in his watch. He had a pet name for her: Belinda.

But he was too shy to express his feelings.

In colonial days, young women often married at age sixteen or seventeen and men at twenty or twenty-one. One reason the colonists married early was that their average life span was less than forty years. It was common for people to die young from diseases and conditions that doctors can cure today. Tom saw his chance to propose marriage at a ball in Williamsburg. But when he danced with Rebecca, he could only say "a few broken sentences," he told a friend. He met her again a few weeks later but only blurted out that he might want to marry her someday. That wasn't much of a proposal! A few months later, Rebecca married another man.

MONTICELLO
"LITTLE MOUNTAIN"

NORTH PAVILION

NORTH TERRACE

ROUNDABOUT

IN ABOUT 1767, JEFFERSON BEGAN DESIGNING MONTICELLO. THE DESIGN RESEMBLED BUILDINGS CREATED BY 16TH-CENTURY ITALIAN ARCHITECT ANDREA PALLADIO. CONSTRUCTION BEGAN IN 1770 AND CONTINUED UNTIL 1809. JEFFERSON MOVED INTO MONTICELLO'S SOUTH PAVILION AFTER HIS BIRTHPLACE, SHADWELL, BURNED TO THE GROUND IN 1770.

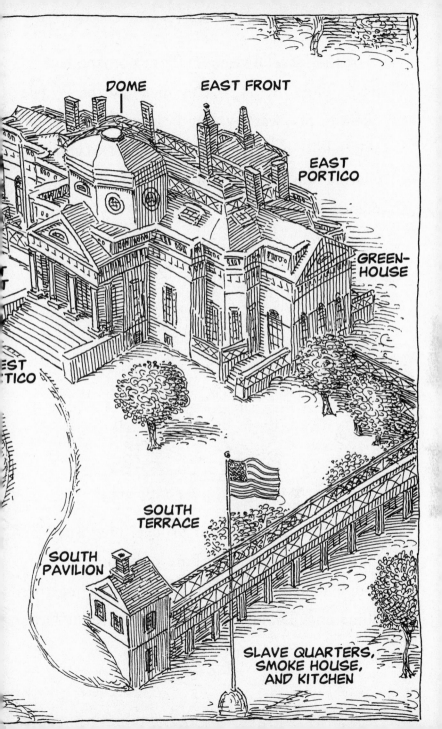

It took several years for Tom's broken heart to heal. Then in 1770, he met Martha Wayles Skelton. She was a young beauty with hazel eyes and reddish brown hair. Just twenty-two years old, Martha was already a widow with a young son named John.

MARTHA WAYLES SKELTON

Martha and Tom fell in love. He visited her father's plantation, The Forest, to court her. The couple shared a love of music. They sang together. Sometimes Thomas played his violin while Martha

played the harpsichord, which resembled a piano. According to a Jefferson family story, one day Thomas and Martha were playing a love song in The Forest's drawing room. Two other admirers of Martha entered the house. Hearing the duet, they knew Thomas had won her heart, so they departed.

On New Year's Day of 1772, Thomas and Martha were married at The Forest. The festivities lasted more than two weeks. On January 18, the

newlyweds set out by buggy for Monticello. They were hit by a blizzard during the 100-mile journey. It was "the deepest snow we have ever seen, about 3 [feet] deep," Thomas wrote in a journal. They had to abandon the buggy and finish the journey on horseback. Not until late at night did the couple arrive at their new home to begin their life together.

Thomas and Martha remained deeply in love during their ten-and-a-half years of marriage. They also endured much sadness together.

Martha's four-year-old son, John, had been left behind at The Forest with his grandparents. John became ill and died in June 1772. Over the next few years, Thomas and Martha had five daughters and a son. All but two of them died before the age of three. Only their firstborn, Patsy, and another daughter, Maria, grew to adulthood.

TOM   PATSY   MARIA   MARTHA

Chapter 3
"We Hold These Truths to Be Self-Evident . . ."

When he married in 1772, Jefferson was in his third year in the House of Burgesses. Over the past few years, the thirteen colonies had grown restless under British rule. England had been trying to tax the colonists. The Americans refused to pay.

Britain's Tea Act of 1773 made things worse. On December 16, a group of people in Boston, Massachusetts, protested this tax on tea. They boarded three ships and dumped 342 chests of tea into Boston Harbor. The tea dumping became known as the Boston Tea Party.

To punish Bostonians, Britain closed the city's harbor. This made it difficult for people in Boston to obtain supplies they needed.

BOSTON TEA PARTY

DECEMBER 16, 1773

TO PROTEST THE TAX ON TEA, PATRIOTS DISGUISED AS NATIVE AMERICANS BOARDED THREE BRITISH SHIPS AND DUMPED 342 CHESTS OF TEA INTO BOSTON HARBOR.

The British hoped the punishment would scare Americans into obeying them. Just the opposite happened. Many colonists, including Thomas Jefferson, were furious. They felt that the unjust British taxes had provoked the Bostonians.

During this time of trouble, Patrick Henry made a famous speech. He said, "Give me liberty or give me death!" Unlike Patrick Henry, Jefferson was a poor speaker. In fact, he often sat silently at public

meetings. But could he write! In 1774, he wrote *A Summary View of the Rights of British America*. This

pamphlet was his first major writing on politics. It revealed that he was thinking of matters far beyond taxes. The colonists might be ready to separate from Britain, he wrote. He even referred to the colonies as the "states of America."

Jefferson had another suggestion. On June 1, 1774—the day Boston's port was to close—the House of Burgesses should not do business as usual. Instead, Virginia lawmakers should pray and fast (not eat) to show support for Massachusetts. Jefferson's fellow lawmakers agreed to his idea.

Lord Dunmore, Virginia's British governor, learned of the plan. He decided to shut down the House of Burgesses in Williamsburg. This didn't

GEORGE
WASHINGTON

stop Thomas Jefferson and his colleagues. They marched to the Raleigh Tavern. There, they declared that Americans were one people and must stick together. They also proposed that a meeting of delegates from all thirteen colonies be organized.

This big meeting was held in Philadelphia, Pennsylvania, in the fall of 1774. It was called the First Continental Congress. Every colony but Georgia sent delegates. Stomach problems kept Jefferson from attending, but Virginia's delegates included George Washington and Patrick Henry. If Britain kept mistreating America, Congress was to meet again the next spring.

Britain didn't change its ways. War between the thirteen colonies and Britain broke out on April 19, 1775, at Lexington, Massachusetts.

The Second Continental Congress opened in Philadelphia at the Pennsylvania State House that May. Jefferson wasn't there at the start, for he had not been chosen as a delegate. But when a vacancy in Virginia's delegation had to be filled, his chance came. Jefferson set out in his buggy on the 250-mile trip to Philadelphia.

BATTLE OF LEXINGTON AND CONCORD
APRIL 19, 1775

By June 22, 1775, the tall, redheaded Virginian had taken his seat in Congress. Although he rarely said a word, everyone knew he had a way with a pen. He was asked to write some of Congress's official documents.

Over the next year, Congress couldn't decide what to do. Some delegates didn't want to cut all ties with Britain. The war that had begun in Massachusetts would soon end, they hoped. Then America would return to British rule. Other delegates, including Thomas Jefferson, wanted to create a new, independent nation. As the war continued, more and more delegates favored independence. On June 7, 1776, Richard Henry Lee of Virginia arose in Congress. Declare America independent, Lee urged.

Congress was to vote on the proposal in early July. A majority of colonies—seven out of thirteen—would have to favor independence for the measure to pass.

What if the vote came out for independence? Then Congress would need to tell the world why America was separating from England. A committee was asked to prepare a Declaration of Independence. Its members were Benjamin

BENJAMIN FRANKLIN

Franklin of Pennsylvania, John Adams of Massachusetts, Roger Sherman of Connecticut, Robert R. Livingston of New York, and Thomas Jefferson of Virginia.

Instead of working as a group, the committee decided that one of them should write the Declaration. Franklin, a world-famous scientist and statesman, seemed like the man for the job. But Ben was seventy years old and not well. Finally, the choice came down to Jefferson or Adams.

This was a difficult time for Thomas. In early 1776, he had been away from Congress, during which time his mother had died. Afterward, Jefferson developed a painful migraine headache that lasted for six weeks. He did not return to Congress until the middle of May. So, on the June day that he talked with John Adams, he was not yet in a writing mood.

Adams later recalled how each of them tried to talk the other into writing the Declaration.

"You ought to do it!" said Jefferson, who at thirty-three was seven years younger than Adams.

"I will not!" John Adams replied.

"Why?" Jefferson wanted to know.

"Reasons enough," said Adams.

"What can be your reasons?" Thomas persisted.

First, explained Adams, a Massachusetts man shouldn't write the Declaration. Massachusetts had been the site of the Boston Tea Party and the war's first battle. Now other colonies should get more involved. Second, the other delegates liked Thomas more than John. A Declaration written by Jefferson would be better received than one by Adams.

"Reason third," said John Adams, "you can write ten times better than I can!"

The praise for his writing did the trick. "Well," said Thomas Jefferson, "if you are decided, I will do as well as I can."

Jefferson sat down in his second-floor apartment at the corner of Philadelphia's Market and Seventh streets. He set up his portable desk and took out paper, pen, and ink. "When in the course of human events," he began, "it becomes necessary

for one people to dissolve the political bands which have connected them with another . . ."

As his pen moved, he became more inspired. A few lines into the Declaration came the stirring words: "We hold these truths to be self-evident, that all men are created equal . . ."

Later he described how England had been mistreating America. He finished with a moving sentence: "And for the support of this Declaration," he concluded, ". . . we mutually pledge to each other our Lives, our Fortunes, and our sacred Honor."

If independence was voted down, the Declaration would go into the garbage. Only if independence passed would the paper be needed. When the vote was made on July 2, twelve colonies chose independence. New York did not

We hold these truths to be self evide that they are endowed by their Creato that among these are life. Liberty

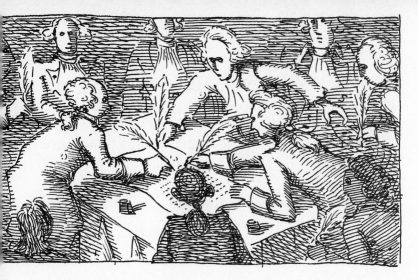

vote. However, several days later New York made the vote unanimous.

The delegates thought that July 2, 1776—when independence was approved—would be considered the new nation's birthday. They were wrong. Congress made some changes in the Declaration, then approved it on July 4. Copies of the Declaration went out to the thirteen new states. Americans loved the paper that proclaimed

that all men are created equal.
with certain inalienable Rights
nd the pursuit of Happiness

their country's birth. Since the document stated, "IN CONGRESS, JULY 4, 1776," on it, Americans began celebrating that date as the nation's birthday. The Fourth of July is honored as the country's birthday to this day.

Did writing the Declaration bring Jefferson instant fame? No. Congress wanted the Declaration to be "an expression of the American mind," as Jefferson put it. No author was named on the document. Until 1784, when a newspaper mentioned it, few people knew that Thomas Jefferson had written the country's "birth certificate."

Chapter 4
Governor and Minister to France

Most members of Congress signed the Declaration on August 2, 1776. Its author signed

the paper *Th Jefferson*. After signing, he was ready to go home. He missed his family. Besides, he felt he was needed in Virginia. He quit his seat in Congress on September 2 and reached Monticello a week later.

In October, Jefferson became a member of Virginia's new state legislature. He served there for three difficult years. England was the world's most powerful nation. For a long while, it appeared that the United States would lose the war.

Jefferson ran for governor of Virginia in June 1779. He was elected and held the office for two years. Jefferson was a brilliant thinker. He was a marvelous writer. But he was not a good wartime governor. Perhaps the biggest problem was that in his heart he was a man of peace. He was not good at raising and arming men for combat. As a result, Virginia was unprepared when the British invaded the state in 1781.

On June 2, 1781, with British forces overrunning Virginia, Jefferson's term as governor ended. Two days later, Jefferson was at Monticello when a messenger arrived with terrible news. The British were coming to capture him! Thomas made Martha and the children board a carriage and escape. He then walked into the woods to see if he could spot the enemy. Seeing no sign of

them, he decided to return home for some papers. Before doing that, he took out a small telescope he had brought along. He aimed it at Charlottesville, just two miles from Monticello. The town was crawling with British troops.

The telescope may have saved his life. The British had seized Monticello. Had he returned home, Jefferson might have been captured and hanged. Instead, he met up with his family.

CONTINENTAL SOLDIER

TRICORN HAT

MUSKET

KNAPSACK

BAYONET

TOMAHAWK

CANTEEN

POWDER HORN

SHOT POUCH

EARLY FLAGS

AN APPEAL TO HEAVEN

LIBERTY

DON'T TREAD ON ME

WHEN THE THIRTEEN COLONIES WENT TO WAR AGAINST ENGLAND, THE AMERICAN COLONISTS WANTED THEIR OWN FLAG TO REPRESENT THE LAND THEY WERE FIGHTING FOR. HERE ARE SOME OF THE FLAGS COLONISTS USED DURING THE REVOLUTION.

Jefferson took them to Poplar Forest, a plantation he owned about eighty miles from Monticello.

A few months after the Jeffersons fled Monticello, the Americans won a stunning victory. It occurred right in Virginia. Ben Franklin had convinced France to help America fight Britain. In October 1781, George Washington's troops, along with French soldiers, crushed the British at Yorktown, Virginia. This victory meant that America had won its war for independence.

BATTLE OF YORKTOWN, OCTOBER 19, 1781

No one was happier about independence than Thomas Jefferson. This should have been a happy time for Jefferson. However, some Virginians accused him of not having done enough earlier as governor to protect the state. Virginia's legislature even held hearings on the subject. Jefferson was cleared of wrongdoing in late 1781. Still, the harsh words from people of his own state hurt him deeply. To make things worse, while horseback riding, Thomas broke his left wrist and suffered other injuries. He couldn't leave the house for six weeks.

In the following year came the worst blow of all. By early 1782, the Jeffersons were back at Monticello. There, on May 8, Martha gave birth to her sixth and last child, Lucy Elizabeth. Martha grew weaker day by day following the birth. For four months, Thomas stayed by her bedside. He read to her from their favorite books. At night, he slept in a nearby room.

In her final hours, Martha told Thomas her last wish. She had three living children—Patsy, Maria, and the baby, Lucy Elizabeth. She couldn't bear for them to be raised by a stepmother. Promise never to remarry, she begged her husband. Thomas promised. A short time later, on September 6, 1782, Martha died.

Thomas's oldest daughter Patsy was nine at the time. Many years later she wrote that her father nearly lost his mind from grief. He would not leave his room for three weeks. When he finally

came out, he went on long horseback rides through the woods. "The violence of his emotion, of his grief," she wrote half a century later, "to this day I dare not trust myself to describe."

Friends such as James Madison thought that Thomas should return to politics. That might take his mind off his grief. Jefferson agreed. In June 1783, Jefferson was elected to the Continental Congress. Over the next six months, he served on nearly every major committee in Congress. He also wrote at least thirty-one government papers.

In the spring of 1784, Congress gave him an important job. He was to go to France and help make treaties with European countries. Jefferson left his two younger daughters with relatives. But

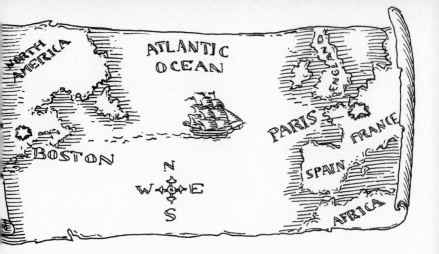

eleven-year-old Patsy made the 3,800-mile voyage with her father. They reached Paris on August 6.

Once he was in France, Jefferson's job changed. Ben Franklin resigned as U.S. minister to France. Jefferson, who had learned some French, was then named to the post. He was to make sure that the United States and France remained friends. He kept in touch with French officials and traveled around the country.

Back home, though, things were going poorly. In October 1784, two-year-old Lucy Elizabeth died of whooping cough. News traveled so slowly by ship that Jefferson didn't find out about it for about three months. The grieving father wanted his only other child, Maria, to join Patsy and himself in France. Eight-year-old Maria was too young to travel alone. Jefferson wrote home asking that one of his slaves sail with her.

A slave named Sally Hemings, only fourteen years old herself, was sent with Maria. The two girls arrived in France in mid-1787. Maria entered the school that Patsy attended. Sally went to work as a house slave in Jefferson's Paris apartment.

SALLY HEMINGS

Sally Hemings was not only a slave. She was closely related to Jefferson's late wife. Martha Jefferson's parents were John and Martha Wayles. Martha's father also had six children with one of his slave women. These children were considered black and were raised as slaves. Sally was one of them. Because they had the same father, Martha and Sally were half-sisters. After John Wayles's death in 1773, Sally had become Martha and Thomas Jefferson's slave at Monticello.

Sally Hemings probably looked like her half-sister. She may have reminded Thomas of Martha in other ways. Jefferson began a relationship with Sally. She had little if any choice in the matter. Because Jefferson was her master, Sally had to do what he wanted. This was just one of the many evil things about slavery. Yet over time, it appears that Sally Hemings and Thomas Jefferson grew very fond of each other. They would maintain their relationship for nearly forty years.

In 1789, Sally Hemings became pregnant. Thomas Jefferson was the father. By then, Jefferson had been overseas for five years. He wanted to go home. Congress said he could. But Jefferson had one problem. Under French law, Sally could become free by staying in France. She agreed to return to the U.S. only if Jefferson made her a promise. Their children had to be freed once they reached adulthood. Sally may have also asked for her own freedom one day as well.

Jefferson agreed. In the fall of 1789, he sailed for home with Sally Hemings and his two daughters. They barely made it. Off Virginia's coast, a storm

lashed their ship, ripping away some of the sails. Then another vessel nearly rammed into them. Their ship also caught fire—but fortunately, just after they had landed.

The travelers reached Monticello two days before Christmas of 1789. Sally's baby was born soon after, but the child seems to have lived only a short time. Jefferson's relationship with Sally continued at Monticello. Over the next nineteen years, they had six more children. Two died in infancy. Their sons Beverley, Madison, and Eston, and their daughter, Harriet, lived to adulthood. Like their mother, these four children were slaves at Monticello.

Many years later, Madison Hemings complained that Thomas Jefferson hadn't shown his slave family any "fatherly affection." However, in one way Jefferson did favor Sally and their children. He saw to it that they had easier jobs than the field slaves. Sally and Harriet did housework and sewing at Monticello. The boys ran errands and worked at carpentry. But they were not free.

Eventually, Sally and her children were given their freedom, but not for many years to come.

Chapter 5
Secretary of State and Vice President

A letter from George Washington awaited Jefferson upon his return home in 1789. That spring, Washington had become our first President. He wanted Jefferson to become his

Secretary of State. This meant that he would head the Department of State, which oversees the United States' relations with other countries. Jefferson wrote back refusing the job. He was now forty-six years old. He hoped to relax for a year. But Washington didn't give up. He sent a second letter. He couldn't do without him, Washington insisted. Jefferson couldn't say no a second time to the hero of the Revolution. He waited until his daughter Patsy was married in February 1790. The next month, he went to New York City—then the nation's capital—to join Washington's cabinet.

Jefferson served as Secretary of State for almost four years. Afraid that spies would open his letters, Jefferson invented a device to keep his messages private. Called a "cipher wheel," it enabled him to write in a secret code.

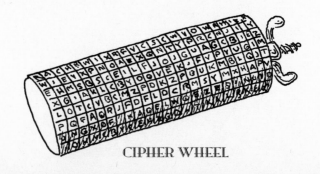

CIPHER WHEEL

As Secretary of State, Jefferson helped the nation avoid conflicts with Britain, France, and Spain. But he and Treasury Secretary Alexander

Hamilton had conflicts of their own. The two men disagreed about the country's future. Hamilton wanted the United States to become a nation of big business and big cities. He favored a strong U.S. government that told the states what they could and couldn't do. Jefferson wanted a nation of small farmers and small towns. He favored a government that stayed out of people's lives as much as possible. The Jefferson-Hamilton clash helped spark the creation of political parties. Jefferson became a leader of the Democratic-Republican Party. Hamilton became a leader of the Federalist Party. We still have two main political parties today. However, they are not the same as those led by Jefferson and Hamilton.

Political differences weren't the only problem between the two men. Jefferson and Hamilton really disliked each other. They argued in cabinet meetings. They fought in the newspapers. Jefferson finally grew weary of the arguing. He resigned from Washington's cabinet at the end of 1793. Early the next year, he returned to Monticello.

Jefferson spent the next three years quietly, at home. He read. He remodeled Monticello, which he continued to do for another fifteen years. He worked at improving his farm. He had his slaves

plant trees, flowers, and various crops. Among his many interests was fossil collecting. He was even nicknamed "Mr. Mammoth" because he gathered fossils of those elephant-like animals of long ago. Jefferson also liked to invent new gadgets. Over the years his creations included a new kind of plow

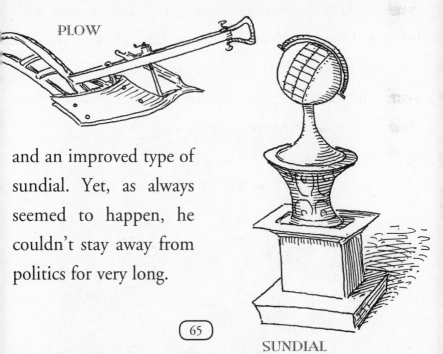

PLOW

and an improved type of sundial. Yet, as always seemed to happen, he couldn't stay away from politics for very long.

SUNDIAL

George Washington retired as President after his second four-year term was over. John Adams, Vice President under Washington, hoped to win the nation's highest office in the 1796 election. Adams became the Federalist candidate. The Democratic-Republicans chose Jefferson.

Rarely has a candidate done so little as Jefferson did in 1796. He made no speeches. Jefferson even told his son-in-law that he wanted John Adams to win.

The election was very close. Adams won with seventy-one electoral votes. According to the law of the time, the person with the second-most votes became Vice President. That was Thomas

Jefferson, with sixty-eight. He moved to Philadelphia, the United States capital, and in 1797 began serving as Vice President.

Jefferson and Adams were old friends. At first they got along well enough. But in time, the President and Vice President clashed. Jefferson was hurt that President Adams didn't even consult him on most issues. To his daughter Patsy, he wrote: "It gives me great regret to be passing my time so uselessly when it could have been so importantly employed at home."

John Adams ran for the presidency again in 1800. So did Thomas Jefferson. And this time, he very much wanted to win.

Chapter 6
Our Third President

The Presidential election of 1800 was bitterly fought. Adams and Jefferson had become enemies. Aaron Burr also sought the Presidency and made backroom deals trying to win. In the end, Thomas Jefferson won, and Aaron Burr was elected Vice President.

Jefferson took office on March 4, 1801. He was the first President inaugurated in Washington, D.C., which had become the nation's permanent capital in 1800. He had been living at a boarding house in Washington. Many people thought he would wear fancy clothes and go by carriage to his inauguration. But on the day he took office, Jefferson dressed plainly. He walked the two blocks from his rooms to the U.S. Capitol

building. There he was sworn in as President.

Jefferson gave a fine speech. A thousand people packed the hall to hear it. Put aside your political differences, the new President told Americans. "We are all Republicans—we are all Federalists."

Jefferson also stated his goal: "Peace . . . and an honest friendship with all nations." The problem was, only the people in the first few rows heard him. He was still a terrible speaker. Besides, he was very nervous. He spoke so quietly, many listeners had to read the speech in the newspapers the next day.

The new President moved into the White House, which wasn't yet completed. Jefferson turned out to be an outstanding national leader. He had long wanted the nation to expand westward. In 1803, he helped make the greatest land deal in U.S. history. For $15 million, the nation bought 828,000 square miles of land from France in what is now the central United States. Called the Louisiana Purchase, this deal doubled the country's size. Later, all or part of fifteen states were carved from the region.

Jefferson was curious about lands beyond the Louisiana Purchase as well. In 1804, he sent out a

THE LEWIS AND CLARK EXPEDITION

MERIWETHER LEWIS

WILLIAM CLARK

THOMAS JEFFERSON HAD ALWAYS BEEN CURIOUS ABOUT THE AMERICAN WEST. AS PRESIDENT, HE COMMISSIONED AN EXPEDITION TO EXPLORE AND MAP THE TERRITORY. IN MAY 1804, CO-CAPTAINS MERIWETHER LEWIS AND WILLIAM CLARK SET OUT FROM NEAR ST. LOUIS, MISSOURI. TRAVELING BY RIVER AND LAND, THEY JOURNEYED TO THE OREGON COAST AND BACK AGAIN—A DISTANCE OF MORE THAN 8,000 MILES. THEY WERE ACCOMPANIED BY A CREW OF MEN—WHICH INCLUDED CLARK'S SLAVE, YORK—AND THE SHOSHONE INDIAN GUIDE AND INTERPRETER, SACAGAWEA. IT TOOK THE EXPLORERS TWO YEARS AND FOUR MONTHS TO COMPLETE THEIR JOURNEY.

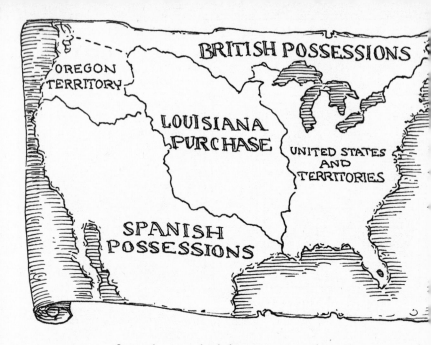

group of explorers led by Meriwether Lewis and William Clark. They traveled from near St. Louis, Missouri, to the Pacific Northwest. On their journey they learned about western lands and Native Americans. The Lewis and Clark Expedition helped the U.S. claim more land. Later, it became three states: Washington, Idaho, and Oregon.

Jefferson brought a new style to the Presidency. Washington and Adams had been formal and dignified. Jefferson was relaxed and friendly. The

THE WHITE HOUSE

THE WHITE HOUSE DURING
JEFFERSON'S TIME

WORK BEGAN ON THE WHITE HOUSE, WHICH WAS TO BE THE HOME OF EACH PRESIDENT, IN 1792. GEORGE WASHINGTON CHOSE THE SITE FOR THE MANSION, BUT HE NEVER LIVED THERE HIMSELF. JOHN ADAMS AND HIS WIFE, ABIGAIL, WERE THE FIRST RESIDENTS—THEY MOVED IN IN LATE 1800. SLAVE LABOR WAS USED TO BUILD THE WHITE HOUSE.

THE WHITE HOUSE TODAY

President rode his horse around Washington, often speaking to strangers. He opened the White House to everyone. "He was dressed with an old brown coat, woolen hose, slippers without heels," wrote one visitor from New Hampshire. "I thought this man was a servant. It was the President." Jefferson's pet mockingbird also surprised visitors. Dick liked to fly about the White House, sometimes landing on Jefferson's shoulder.

Jefferson was re-elected as President in late 1804. This time, George Clinton of New York was his Vice President. By his second inauguration, Jefferson was sixty-one years old. He was a grandfather now. Sometimes his loved ones from Virginia visited him in Washington. During one visit, in early 1806, Patsy had her eighth child. The baby was named James Madison Randolph. James was the first baby born in the White House.

President Jefferson also kept in touch with his family by writing letters. On his second inauguration day—March 4, 1805—Jefferson wrote to his granddaughter Ellen. The "pressure of the day" made it hard for him to write a long letter, he explained. But he sent her a poem. He ended by saying:

> *I am called [away] by company. Therefore, God bless you, my dear child. Kiss your Mama and sisters for me, & tell them I shall be with them in about a week from this time.*
>
> *Th. Jefferson*

Jefferson expected his grandchildren to write back to him.

Ellen didn't answer Jefferson's March 4 letter. So, later that spring, he wrote to her, saying, that if she didn't write soon, "I shall send the sheriff after you." The nine-year-old girl knew that her grandfather the President was joking, but she did write back.

Keeping peace was the greatest challenge of President Jefferson's second term. The British needed sailors for their ships. They often got them by stopping American vessels at sea and kidnapping American sailors. To make things worse, Britain attacked the U.S. Navy ship *Chesapeake* in 1807. Jefferson ordered British ships out of American waters. He resisted the outcry to take revenge on Britain, however. By so doing, he kept the nation out of war.

As President, he also considered ways to end slavery. The man who had declared that "all men are created equal" knew that slavery was wrong. He once wrote: "Nothing is more certainly written in the book of fate, than that these people [the slaves] are to be free." And as far back as 1774, he had said that freeing the slaves was "the great object of desire" in the thirteen colonies. He also saw that he was part of the problem. Over the years, he had owned 400 slaves at Monticello, including Sally Hemings and the four children they had together.

Jefferson considered ways to end slavery. Should all the slaves be freed at once? Should they be freed gradually? Or was it best just to prevent new slaves from entering the country? Freeing all the slaves at once would cause problems, he thought. A slave was worth hundreds of dollars, a lot of money in those days. Southern whites might be fighting mad if their slaves were freed.

He finally acted in 1806, but with a weak attack on slavery. That December, President Jefferson asked Congress to end the slave trade. As of January 1, 1808, it became illegal to bring any more slaves into the country. Jefferson hoped that this would make slavery slowly die out. But it didn't. New slaves were smuggled in. And slaves already in America had children. These babies were born into slavery, increasing the slave population. Jefferson's failure to act boldly to end slavery was perhaps his greatest failure as President. Not until 1865 would the Civil War end slavery in the United States.

Jefferson probably could have won a third term. But, like George Washington, he thought two terms were enough. During his second term, he also suffered from terrible headaches that kept

him from working for days at a time. He decided not to run again in 1808. He was pleased when his friend James Madison succeeded him as President.

JAMES MADISON

On the March day in 1809 that he took office, Madison asked Jefferson to ride with him in his carriage. Jefferson refused, wanting no special treatment. "This day, I return to the people," he said.

Former President Jefferson then went home to Monticello.

Chapter 7
Last Years at Monticello

Jefferson was nearly sixty-six when he retired to Monticello. He spent the last seventeen years of his life at the home he loved.

The year her father returned, Patsy moved to Monticello with her husband and children. Of Patsy's twelve sons and daughters, all but one reached adulthood. Jefferson's daughter Maria had died. But her son, Francis, who was seven years old when Jefferson retired, was often at Monticello.

Jefferson loved nothing more than to pass the

time with his grandchildren. Grandpapa Jefferson played the violin for them while they danced. He ran races with them on the lawn. He enjoyed giving them books and other presents. His granddaughter Ellen received a special gift. Jefferson gave her the portable desk on which he had written the Declaration of Independence.

PORTABLE WRITING DESK

When away from his grandchildren, Jefferson wrote to them. In a letter to his granddaughter Cornelia, he pointed out that she should remember her periods and capital letters while writing. He included a little rhyme to show what he meant:

I've seen the sea all in a blaze of fire
I've seen a house high as the moon and higher
I've seen the sun at twelve o'clock at night
I've seen the man who saw this wondrous sight.

Jefferson wanted his granddaughter to see that this only makes sense if punctuated properly:

I've seen the sea. All in a blaze of fire
I've seen a house. High as the moon and higher
I've seen the sun. At twelve o'clock at night
I've seen the man who saw this wondrous sight.

Nine-year-old Cornelia Jefferson Randolph wrote back to her grandfather:

> *Dear Grandpapa*
>
> *I hope you will excuse my bad writing, for it is the first letter I ever wrote, there are a number of faults, in it I know but those you will excuse; I am reading a very pretty little book, I am very much pleased with it. all the children send their love to you we all want to see you very much. adieu my dear Grandpapa, believe me to be your most affectionate Granddaughter. C.R.*

Jefferson complained to his grandchildren if they didn't answer his letters. In turn, they teased him if he didn't answer theirs. In 1813, eleven-year-old Francis wrote:

> *Dear Grandpapa*   *April 1813*
>
> *I wish to see you very much I am very sorry that you wont write to me this leter will make twice I have wrote to you and if you dont answer this leter I shant write to you any more . . .*

Actually, Jefferson rarely failed to answer a letter.

He wrote 36,000 letters in his lifetime. In those days, most people made copies of their letters by hand. Jefferson had a device that made copies for him as he wrote. It was a special desk with several pens attached by wires. As he used one pen, the others moved automatically and copied his letter. Although he hadn't invented this device, he did make improvements to it.

THE EARLY POST OFFICE

IN 1789, CONGRESS CREATED THE UNITED STATES POST OFFICE AS PART OF THE FEDERAL GOVERNMENT. POSTAGE RATES WERE FIXED ACCORDING TO THE DISTANCE THAT THE MAIL TRAVELED AND THE NUMBER OF PAGES BEING SENT. MOST PEOPLE COLLECTED THEIR MAIL AT THE NEAREST POST OFFICE (OFTEN THE LOCAL TAVERN OR GENERAL STORE), BUT A 1794 ACT DID PERMIT HOME DELIVERY FOR TWO CENTS EXTRA PER LETTER. IN EITHER CASE, THE PERSON WHO RECEIVED THE MAIL WAS RESPONSIBLE FOR PAYING THE POSTAGE, RATHER THAN THE SENDER.

Many of his letters were to another former President. By 1811, Jefferson and John Adams hadn't spoken in ten years. Friends convinced them to make up. In 1812, when Adams was seventy-six and Jefferson sixty-eight, they began exchanging letters. The two men discussed religion, politics, even whether they would want to go back in time and live their lives differently. Across 500 miles— John Adams was in Massachusetts and Jefferson in Virginia—they wrote back and forth until nearly the end of their lives.

In his last years, Jefferson also achieved an old dream. He had long planned to start a new university in Virginia. For the school's site, he chose Charlottesville, near his home. He helped raise money for the school, chose most of its teachers, and planned its courses. Jefferson was a fine architect. Now, with his granddaughter Cornelia helping him, he designed the buildings for the new university. Cornelia, a gifted artist, was

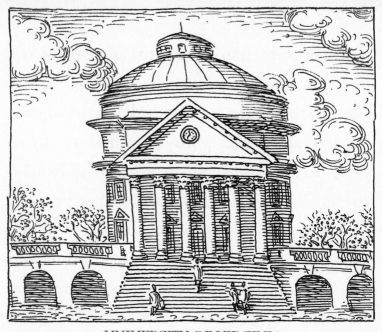

UNIVERSITY OF VIRGINIA

only about twenty at the time. Jefferson was almost eighty-two when the school he founded, the University of Virginia, opened in 1825. Its campus is still one of the most beautiful in the United States.

Yet, unfortunately, throughout these years Jefferson had money trouble. Upon retiring as President, he had borrowed $8,000 to pay his debts in Washington. Things got worse at

Monticello. In 1815, he raised money by selling his books to the government. The 6,000 volumes became the core for the Library of Congress.

The book sale helped for a while. But crop failures, a flood, and a loan to a friend hurt his finances. By January 1826, Jefferson couldn't pay his grocery bills. He was $100,000 in debt. That would be equal to about $2 million in today's money. It appeared that he might have to sell Monticello. Donations from friends and even from strangers prevented his total ruin.

Still, as long as his family was nearby and he had books to read, Jefferson was satisfied. And he

remained in good health into his early eighties. He rode his horse, Eagle, for an hour or two on most days. But as his eighty-third birthday approached, Jefferson was slipping. By February, he was in bed much of the time. His family could see that he didn't have much longer to live.

On July 2, Jefferson gathered his loved ones to his bedside. They must live honest and good lives in his memory, he said. But he still had one last wish. He wanted to live until a special day. As the hours passed he kept asking, "Is this the Fourth? Is this the Fourth?"

The day he was awaiting finally arrived. Early that afternoon, eighty-three-year-old Thomas Jefferson took his last breath. By an amazing coincidence, that same day ninety-year-old John Adams also passed away in Massachusetts.

Both men died on July 4, 1826—the fiftieth anniversary of the Declaration of Independence.

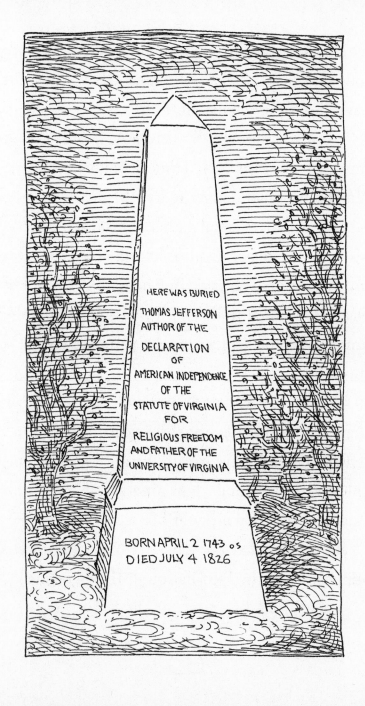

Chapter 8
Thomas Jefferson's Legacy

Jefferson kept his promise to Sally Hemings. All four of their children were freed while Jefferson was still living or by the terms of his will. Their son Beverley and daughter Harriet settled in Washington, D.C. Madison moved to Ohio, earning a living as a farmer and carpenter. Eston, a professional violinist, lived in Ohio and then Wisconsin. Sally Hemings was freed soon after Jefferson's death. She settled in Charlottesville, Virginia, and lived to age sixty-two. Jefferson's daughter Patsy had thirty-two grandchildren and survived to age sixty-four.

Monticello was neglected for many years after Jefferson's death. In 1923, the home was bought by a group that restored it. Today it is open to visitors from all over the world who want to know about Jefferson and his times.

Across America, towns, parks, and other landmarks have been named for Thomas Jefferson. Since 1938, our third President has been pictured on the front of U.S. nickels. Jefferson's home, Monticello, appears on the back of these five-cent coins. The Jefferson Memorial in Washington, D.C., opened on April 13, 1943—his 200th birthday. It has a statue of Jefferson and selections from his writings. In 1941, work was completed on the Mount Rushmore National Memorial in

MOUNT RUSHMORE

South Dakota. This huge sculpture portrays four great Presidents: George Washington, Thomas Jefferson, Theodore Roosevelt, and Abraham Lincoln.

There is also a national holiday associated with Jefferson. Most Americans call it the Fourth of

July. Some call it Independence Day. It is the birthday of the Declaration of Independence— and of the country Thomas Jefferson helped to create.

Th Jefferson

Jefferson's Sayings and Expressions

Like Benjamin Franklin, Jefferson liked to use expressions and catchy sayings, some of which he coined. Here are a few:

"Resistance to tyrants is obedience to God."
    —A favorite saying of T.J.'s

"It is wonderful how much may be done if we are always doing."
    —From a letter to his daughter, Patsy, May 5, 1787

"A mind always employed is always happy."
    —To Patsy, May 21, 1787

"None of us, no not one, is perfect."
    —To Patsy, July 17, 1790

"Delay is preferable to error."
    —From a letter to George Washington, May 16, 1792

"Hope is so much pleasanter than despair."
    —From a letter to his granddaughter, Ellen, June 29, 1807

Bibliography

Boykin, Edward. **To the Girls and Boys: Letters of Thomas Jefferson to and from His Children and Grandchildren.** New York: Funk & Wagnalls, 1964.

Brodie, Fawn M. **Thomas Jefferson: An Intimate History.** New York: Norton, 1974.

Donovan, Frank. **Mr. Jefferson's Declaration.** New York: Dodd, Mead, 1968.

Fleming, Thomas. **The Man from Monticello: An Intimate Life of Thomas Jefferson.** New York: Morrow, 1969.

Gordon-Reed, Annette. **Thomas Jefferson and Sally Hemings: An American Controversy.** Charlottesville: University Press of Virginia, 1997.

Lengyel, Cornel Adam. **The Declaration of Independence.** New York: Grosset & Dunlap, 1968.

Smith, Page. **Jefferson: A Revealing Biography.** New York: American Heritage, 1976.

TIMELINE OF JEFFERSON'S LIFE

1743 —— Born on April 13 at Shadwell

1752 —— Sent to study with Reverend William Douglas

1757 —— Jefferson's father, Peter Jefferson, dies

1760 —— Enrolls at the College of William and Mary

1769 —— Wins a seat in the House of Burgesses

1770 —— Shadwell burns down; Construction of Monticello begins

1772 —— Marries Martha Wayles Skelton

1774 —— Writes the pamphlet *A Summary View of the Rights of British America*

1775 —— Elected to the Second Continental Congress; American Revolution begins

1776 —— Writes the Declaration of Independence

1779 —— Elected governor of Virginia

1782 —— Martha Jefferson dies

1784 —— Replaces Ben Franklin as U.S. minister to France, moves to Paris

1789 —— Sally Hemings, one of Jefferson's slaves, becomes pregnant with their first child together

1790 —— Becomes Secretary of State

1796 —— Becomes Vice President of the United States

1801 —— Sworn into office as President of the United States on March 4

1803 —— The United States acquires the Louisiana Purchase

1804 —— The Lewis and Clark Expedition is launched; Jefferson is re-elected President

1809 —— Retires to Monticello

1815 —— Sells his book collection to the government

1825 —— Founds the University of Virginia, designed by Jefferson and his granddaughter Cornelia

1826 —— Dies at Monticello on July 4, the fiftieth anniversary of the Declaration of Independence

Timeline of The World

Princeton University is founded	1747
The waltz becomes a popular dance in Europe	1750
Chinese invade and conquer Tibet	1752
The historic Liberty Bell is hung at Independence Hall in Philadelphia	1753
Boston Tea Party	1773
Louis XVI becomes king of France	1774
The American Revolution begins; the city of San Francisco is founded	1775
Astronomer Frederick William Herschel discovers the planet Uranus	1781
The first successful hot-air balloon flight is recorded in Paris	1783
The first steamboat is built	1787
George Washington is elected as the first President of the United States; the French Revolution begins	1789
Johnny Appleseed plants apple trees in the Ohio Valley	1801
Webster's Dictionary is first published	1806
Louisiana becomes the eighteenth state in the Union	1812
Francis Scott Key writes "The Star Spangled Banner"	1814
Spain cedes Florida to the United States	1819
The Missouri Compromise: Missouri is admitted to the United States as a slave state, but slavery is barred in the rest of the Louisiana Purchase	1820
Beethoven writes Symphony No. 9	1823
The first U.S. railway is constructed in Massachusetts	1826